CROSSING

by John Matthias

Bucyrus (1970)
23 Modern British Poets (*ed.*, 1971)
Turns (1975)
Introducing David Jones (*ed.*, 1979)
Five American Poets (*ed.*, 1979)
Contemporary Swedish Poetry (*translations*, with
    Göran Printz-Påhlson, 1979)

John Matthias
Crossing

THE **SWALLOW PRESS** INC.
CHICAGO

Published by
The Swallow Press Incorporated
811 W. Junior Terrace
Chicago, Illinois 60613

First Printing 1979

Library of Congress Catalog Card Number: 79-65244
ISBN 0-8040-0829-9 cloth
ISBN 0-8040-0830-2 paper

For Lois Kirkpatrick Matthias
and Pamela Adams

*

And for a house:
Cherry Tree
Hacheston, Suffolk

Contents

III   The Stefan Batory and Mihail Lermontov Poems

I Remainders

In Memory of the American Fifties

Where have they gone –
Those adolescent girls
I loved but never touched?
The ones with clear complexions,
Perfect legs, and breasts
I stared at over shelves of
Magazines in shops: All
The high-jumping cheerleaders,
The handsome homecoming queens.
Did they fit too well their sweaters,
Fit too well those parts
They played in 1956 when
Foster Dulles spoke of reappraisals
And when, agonizing,
Robert Lowell quoted him?

There were others –
Those who had no partners
At the dances but pretended
To be interested in conversation
Or in cokes while all their
Sexy sisters felt the cocks
That swelled against their legs
When lights were low.
Those girls who sat in corners
Have grown lithe and tough: they'll
Race this wanton world to its end.
Among the dancers, though,
Who survives the dance?
Did they die at twenty-nine,
O all of them?
Or did you marry one, my friend,
Perhaps the very last,
Who winds her hair in curlers now
And drinks her whisky straight –
Who leaves you home alone at night
And stays out very late?

On Lake Michigan – I

Just after dawn we left the cabin
      to walk on the beach in the wind.
Your hair blew in front of you –
      over your head and across your cheek.
The breakers were high & violent.
      That's again the way I was in the night –
High and violent, breaking . . .

We climbed the dunes on Saltar's point
      saying nothing, waking up.
Soon the heavy mist had soaked us both.
      Your sweater clung against your
Breasts, nipples large & dark – nipples of
      a swollen woman soon to nurse.
I wiped the water from my arm and blew
      it off my fingers like a kiss.
You laughed and ran out knee-deep in the surf.

Here before the fire I write it down.
      Then I read some simple, perfect
Poems by someone else and wonder once again
      if ever I'll be any good at
Writing or at living. You bring me sausages
      and eggs who manage to do everything
So simply and so well. The water drips
      from your hair & you smile.

(1968)

On Lake Michigan – II
(Sinai, Biafra, Pakistan)

Twenty degrees below the normal for May,
    a heavy mist and fierce wind off the lake:
I cut up logs for the iron pot-bellied stove.
    We came here thinking *enough, enough*
(Of Winter & its deaths), and now my daughters
    both are ill, sweating out their fevers
In their sleeping bags . . .

For days they've complained of the smell:
    Alewives in thousands wash up nightly
On the beach. Early every morning I've buried
    these small, grey fish in piles, clearing
The distance for games . . . graves everywhere, mounds,
    holding my nose. Doing that, I easily
Forgot those others digging too, though they were not
    nearby . . . And digging

Not in campgrounds, but in towns; not on private beaches
    but on beach heads; and not to bury Alewives
But to bury wives – husbands, daughters, sons –
    under the sand, under the earth with
Them all . . . Even now, kindling wood to keep
    sick children warm, making awkward
Hands do unfamiliar things a hundred miles from
    a telephone or car, I can easily forget
Enough to think I bring on spring instead of fire.

In Columbus, Ohio

Cautiously, hoping that nobody sees,
    I stop my hired car outside your house.
You are not there, but far away
    in California putting your children to bed –
Nor have I seen you once in fifteen years.
    It's past eleven: your mother's floating by
A window in a purple robe, your father's
    reading a book. They have both been sick.
Like all their friends, they've had their
    operations, retired from their jobs, and begun,
To their annoyance, talking – like any poet –
    of the past.

What if we had married? The notion seems
    outrageously absurd, and yet, before our lives
Began in earnest, that, as I recall, was once
    indeed the plan. For years, I preferred your
House to mine, your parents to my own. . . .
    And then I loathed them, thought these shadows
At the window pane were guilty of offences
    intellectual and moral, that they drove you
Crazy to extremes of anarchy and lust through
    their chaste example & their discipline when
All the virginal austerity was mine.

What I want to do, you see, is to leap from
    the car, pound on the door, and say:
Forgive me! as they stand there staring in the
    autumn night. . . . (Perhaps we'd spend
An hour drinking brandy then, and tell long tales,
    and show each other photographs,
And shake hands solemnly at twelve. . . .) But
    of course I don't do anything like
That at all. I start the car and drive on East
    as far as Philadelphia.

A Reply

('Sir: I am collecting poems relating to the late John Berryman for an anthology to be published next year, A Tumult for John Berryman'*)*

Oh no, let's not be tumultuous;
Try *serene,* try *gentle*
After all. Sane and boring maybe
At the end I hoped
He'd be – Old and hoary like some
Ancient stoic laureate
Who fakes senility in order
To survive – and manages,
And lasts it out.

At the funeral of tenderness
He thought he walked; let's
Have a little then –
Of tenderness, and
Some respect. Because beyond the tumult
And the swagger – deep inside
That house that Henry built – there
Sat down once, serene, a free
And gentle man.

U.S.I.S. Lecturer
— *Amsterdam, Kalverstraat, March*

What I hear at first is *Heren* and then *Heroine*.
Then the sudden toothy Dutchman
Ages dreadfully and vaguely threatens
Something, turns American,
And says with perfect clarity: "Heroin,

Like *smack*." We stare each other down.
Eyes gone, muscles gone, he is teeth & yellow paper.
Still, I sense he is about my age.
I brush on past him, mind all wheeling
Backwards out of gear

To 1961 when I was here before and just eighteen.
What I dreamed into the streets of Amsterdam
Was Love: pure, high, unyielding,
Disdainful, and serene.
An appallingly beautiful bawd said she'd

Take my friend and me together. He
Went in alone, and for a moment I could see
Them swimming in the gaudy lights
Behind her fishbowl window. Someone opened up
A paper and I read: *Hemingway Zelfmoord*.

A decade and a half. I'm here to lecture twice
On a man who was my teacher once
Who, that very afternoon, in hot America,
Sat down aching and wrote out:
"My mother has your shotgun." And:

"It's so I broke down here."
In the middle of his poem, he meant.
I heard myself quote Woody Allen to a group
Of students yesterday in Leiden when
They asked me what I thought they could believe in.

Sex and death, I said.
Part of me's gone rotten as my junkie-brother's eyes.
Respectful and respectable, I took
A check from my ambassador
And quoted Woody Allen's quip to get a laugh.

I forgot to say: "*It was as he wrote his poem,*
You understand. His father
Had selfmurdered too." Somewhere there,
In 1961 or so, was Love.
I'll think about the man who wrote the poem.

Elegy for Clara

I remember milkweed at the shore
and cattail stems which I was
lacing absent-mindedly through oarlocks
of the dinghy when I noticed you,
sensual and vulnerable, even
to my inexperienced eyes, a lock of reddish hair
matted at the crotch of your bikini
as you lay there smiling,
sunning on your cousin Cherubini's
new, expensive dock. You looked me over
like you would a flock of hens.
You were The Older Sister of
my new impressive friend, and the setting was
from some bad movie none of us
had seen: the private island and the bathing beach,
the sailboat and the sea.
In the night, your cousin's guests
would all sing barbershop quartets
because your father was insistent that we should –
and every moon
must rhyme with June
and like it.
You were a reticent and recent bride
and it was late September.

In the Winter, my poor red ears aflame,
infected by the complications
of the February strep, I heard
the gossips saying "Terrible! it's awful"
and I thought at first they meant
the pain I felt. I saw them, bleary, wagging
fingers with my mother by the kitchen sink
where she poured me out
a draught of Nelson's Balsam recommended
by a British shrink we knew.
They said the man who'd married you

demanded you do "awful things"
and so you left him
like you should have – fast –
because one doesn't have to stomach *that*.
I was too terrified and sick
to ask them what they meant, though
I thought I'd die to know it
or else heal.
I stuffed the cotton deeper in my ears
and thought about it off and on
for twenty years.
For twenty years you spent
your life alone not far from Cherubini's island.

Clara, ageless Older Sister,
I must have thought you were immortal.
Are you really dead at forty-three who wouldn't
have remembered me, my
roving child's eye, the cotton
in my red, infected ears,
who heard the gossips talking and despaired?
Can you accept a stranger's elegy?
I send no flowers
and I do not talk to mourners at your wake
about the things one doesn't have to stomach
or the things that one must take.
I throw no clod of earth onto your grave.
But I am absolutely certain that I loved you once.
And I remember milkweed at the shore
and cattail stems in oarlocks
of the dinghy by that dock
at Cherubini's island in September.

Poem for Cynouai

i

With urgency and passion you argue for the lot –
every one of thirty water colours
ranged in retrospective
which I thought to choose among.
Circumspect, I sought
negotiations. You squint your lazy eye
and wave your arm in arcs
around our geocentric circle and insist:
"We'll take them all!"

ii

I am easily persuaded.
How luminous their rendering of a world
we both believe in
and can sometimes share: –
where names are properties of things
they name, where stones
are animate and wilful, trees
cry out in storms, and compulsive
repetition of the efficacious formulae
will get us each his way.

When they patched your overcompensating eye
your work began. Your starboard
hemisphere was starved for colours
and for shapes.
Suddenly a punning and holistic
gnostic, you painted
everything in sight:
your left eye flashed at cats & camels
in the clouds, while one by one
you drew them with a shrewd right hand
into a white corral.

At school they said your "problem"
was "perceptual".

            iii

What did you perceive,
and what did I?
I found that scattering of words
in notes. I wrote it down
two years ago and now you do not paint.
I no longer wrote. It's out
of date, we've changed.
I was going to quote Piaget
and go on to talk about perception.
Instead I went to work
and earned some money, girl.
I was going to call
you *child*.

Two years, then. We'll keep it honest
as I wander back with you
to Shelford. Bob & Earlene live in Shelford
now, Leif and Luke and Kristin.
Bob has poems in which
he whispers *child*, *child*.
"We'll take them all", you said,
and I said
I am easily persuaded.
We took just one.

            iv

But it is altogether marvelous.
I've kept it here while
you've gone riding with your friends.
Your passion now is horses.
It feels as if you've been away two years –
two years.

Stout-hearted Moshe,
peering one-eyed through your
horse's ears, this bright Ikon that
you've left me makes me
think of William Blake's *Glad Day*.
One sad poet wrote: My
daughter's heavier. And another:
O may she be beautiful, but
not *that* beautiful. I have a friend
who's visited Ms Yeats –
She's bald with warts! O daughters
and their bright glad days
growing beautiful or heavier or bald.
O foolish leers and Lears.

We played. And we play now, but
not so much. Our problem
was perceptual. I think we were
perhaps too Japanese:
I have it on authority
that formal speech retains
the spirit of *bushido* in Japan.
In the *asobase-Kotoba*
we don't say: "I'm here in Shelford"
or "You're riding"
but: "I pretend to be in Shelford"
and "You play at
going riding." Nor does one say:
"I hear your father's dead",
but this instead:
"I understand your father
has played dying."

v

When my father finished playing dying
I began.
You gave me pictures

22

which I held against a wound.
I wrote: "How luminous their rendering
of a world we both believe in"
and then I think you stopped believing . . .

For money, with a friend,
I helped to translate Lars Noren
who far away
in dark, cold Sweden wrote:

Today I see that my daughter
is higher, greater
than I, and completed . . . Her
hard kaiser head encircles me & carries
me and helps me. Silently
we speak in each other — Then
she paves the dead ones.
She comes towards me in her kaiser skirt.

How I stumbled after you with memories & books.
How far ahead you rode. How very
quickly all the books
were closed. How frightening the horses are

As you approach me on The Black Duke of Norfolk.
The Duke's Funeral Helm is low on your eyes
(I stole it for you from a golden nail
in Framlingham church).
Your Ming Dynasty jodhpurs cling to your legs,
cling to your horse's sides
(I sent for them express to Rajasthan).
Your Dalai Lama coat is zipped up tight
(I zipped it up myself).
Your green Tzarina vest divests me.
Your beady Pony Club badge is a third eye
pinned to your cheating heart.
On a velvet photograph of Princess Anne
you are riding in circles of dust.

One eye is patched, old pirate,
and the other eye is glazed.
Only the third one, the Pony Club badge,
can see me, and it stares,
fiery and triumphant.
You are riding in circles of dust.
You are riding into the eye of the Pony Club badge.

First they patched your eye
and then I saw.
My problem was perceptual.

Lars Noren concludes:
She hungers after herself. . . .

    vi

What I had wanted to say was: *red, ocher,*
orange, blue, green, violet.
What I had wanted to say was: *grass, sky,*
sun, moon, child, forest, sea.
I had wanted to say: *English village.*
I had wanted to say:
English village a long time ago . . .
What I had wanted to hear
was the music of flutes and recorders
in a summer garden –
flutes and recorders and tambourines . . .

What I had wanted to see was light
filtering through the trees
deep in a forest near the sea
where elves and children play together
and adults sip tea
by an enormous ornamented samovar
in solemn conversation
on the nature of the games
the elves & children play . . .

What I had wanted to write was
love, immortal, laughter, wings . . .
What I had wanted to do
was to walk forever into a vision
painted by my daughter.
I had wanted her to take me with her there.
I had wanted her
to close the door behind us . . .

    vii

Made of blues and ochers, greens,
made of sunrise and of grass & sky & trees –
Which will be the day
that you remember, child,
when I am only soul-stuff
and can no more enjoy this awkward body
which, despite its ills,
manages to do extraordinary simple things
like walk through heaths of gorse
with you before the others are awake
as the sun comes over
the edge of the earth the ships fall off of
as they tilt on their keels
and roll on the world's last wave . . .

I remember a day: the rowboat rocked
in the reeds:
my father watched his line. All
the night before we had slept together
in a shack waiting for the dawn.
We didn't talk for hours. He, for once,
was beautifully distracted from
what he always called "the difficult business
of living." There was
no past, there was no future there
in those reeds . . .
                      we were adrift in time,

in timelessness
and no one said we must return –

nor did we sail over any edge of any earth.

Or again: near the house of my childhood
on a street called Glen Echo Drive
there was a tree, an oak,
where my father swung me in a swing –
his long thin fingers
and his firm damp palms on the small of my back
I feel still –
and my bare & grimy feet going up through the leaves!

Mosses grow between his fingers now
and along his palms.
Mosses grow in his mouth & under his arms.
When he finished playing dying
I began . . .
You gave me pictures
which I held against a wound.
I wrote: *How luminous their rendering* as

You came toward me saying *muzzle, poll, crest,
withers, loins, croup, dock* . . .
As you came saying *snaffle, whip, spurs,
pommel, cantle, girth.*

     viii

And so I try to learn new words
like any child –
I say *flank, hock, heel, hoof*;
I say *fetlock, gaskin, thigh, stifle, sheath.*
I would meet you now
according to my bond. I try to put away
this Ikon which sustained me.

I write *Equitation: Mounting & dismounting.*
Circumspect, I seek
negotiations. I wave my arms
around in frantic circles and insist:
"I'll learn them all"
while you ride off on paths
through fields of gorse and into sunsets
which are not even slightly picturesque –

While you ride off in hurricanes of dust.

– Just one time were three of us together:
father, father-son, and daughter.
We played at something, riding, painting,
poetry, or dying –
it hardly matters what . . .
And at our playing
                              – (while, perhaps,
someone picked a mandolin
and strangers talked about us solemnly
around an ornamented samovar
and sipped their tea) –
our lines of vision crossed
and then we started changing places painfully . . .

The child is father of the man
but not the child the poet meant.
The child of flesh and blood
and not the ghost of former selves
is father of the man –
The Daughter on the Black Duke of Norfolk
She
is father of the man
The Daughter
Who is Higher, Greater & Completed
She
is father of the man
The Daughter on the Black Duke of Norfolk

The one who made the picture
the one who gave the gift
the one who paved the dead
the one who wore the patch
the one who was Japanese
the one who learned to ride a horse
And Hungers After Herself —

She
is father of the man
The daughter on the Black Duke of Norfolk

The one whose problem was perceptual

The one who rides away

> And the Manual says: *It is interesting to assess the progress and accuracy of the training by riding a circle on ground upon which the imprints of the horse's hoofs can be seen . . .*

(1974–1977)

II Sums

Double Invocation
as a Prologue to a Miscellany of Poems
Mostly Written in East Anglia

i

. . . dRex, dregs, up & out
of the past
by the golden spurs

why not? & drags
him out from under
the bridge

from out of his grave
his marbles intact
and his relics in France

undRex, Edmund Rex
commander Rex
commando and King

and saint! all man
all mundo, myth
and sick of it too

bones in a basket
Abbo's Rex, Ailwin's Rex
and the tourist's:

this is the place
and this is
I truly apologize

only a space I must
clear to begin
& ask for your help

too looming a figure
I know it
but how could I

possibly choose
anyone else
for a guide without

losing my way? Edmund
King and Martyr,
Edmund, King of the bean?

ii

A word about Danes is also in order
to make a beginning
to get under way, but who

would put in a word, a good word
for the Danes?
Barbarous heathens you'd say

with curious names like Ubba
& Hingwar & Sweyn
the patricide killer of Blodrand

Sweyn, whose heir was Cnut – I've
spelled it correctly –
Cnut was a King and a Christian

to moot a point.
But I don't know about Danes.
Once I had an *au pair*

and she was a Dane.
I don't think she was Christian –
large and marvelous tits

I kissed them once in a car
being drunk
though I never saw her Cnut

and one of my closest friends
is a Swede
which is almost a Dane

with a name like Ubba or Sweyn.
Ulfkettle may have com-
manded the army against them in 869.

That would have been against Hingwar.
Did Turchil stand against Sweyn?
I don't know very much about Danes

but O what a lovely girl, my friend,
a calamitous coast,
the wuthering troubles in store!

The Fen Birds' Cry

i

Would you take a caul
along to the sea
it prevents drowning

It shines at birth
prevents
your ship from sinking

On heads of the lucky
a membrane
it makes the solicitor grave

Endows with gift of argument
brings wealth
or would you hold

Hard to the hands of the dead.

ii

Would you hold hard to the hands
of the dead
a minute a minute a minute

Or take from the forehead a florin
there where the handywoman
put it the corpse money the florin

Would you have no child for a year
would you take
a caul along to the sea

Prevent drowning prevent
a ship from sinking & make a solicitor
grave would you hold

Hard to the hands of the dead.

Evening Song

Evening: and we
    wait for a train to pass
And my daughter
    says she sees the
Guard's van
    coming round the bend
A quarter of a mile
    or so away.

You mean
    the caboose . . .
I say & she looks happily
    and firmly
At the guard's van
    and pulls
At white cow parsley
    by the fence at the edge
Of the tracks
    that William Carlos
Williams
    in America called
Queen Anne's
    Lace. There's nothing
Royal at all
    about the stuff in Suffolk.

Evening. Laura pulls at
    cow parsley: we
Await the rolling guard's van.
    We live here.

Somewhere in Ohio
 the lantern on the back
Of the world's
 reddest last caboose
Vanishes
 down singing rails
Into the darkness
 of my
  childhood.

Two Ladies

So many incorrupt bodies, such
Corrupting times!
Edmund to and fro for years,

Inspected, found intact,
Unburied & unbothered & unblemished
And then, then these ladies

These incorruptible ladies
Like Etheldreda Queen & Sainted Audrey
Earlier than Edmund even

Wearing round her neck a fabled string
Of beads that purpled flesh
Into a fatal tumor that she liked:

She had, she said, been vain.
Daughter of the hypothetical incumbent
Of the ship at Sutton Hoo,

Daughter of the priest who taught her,
Touchy and untouched –
By Tondbert Prince of Fenmen and

By Ecgfrith son of Osway the Northumbrian –
She ruled, queened, twice,
And got sick of it, of royalty, and fled:

Fled to Abbess Eba, solicitous and grave,
Where randy Ecgfrith followed
With his louts who'd leered at her around

The smutty fire inside the great log hall.
Flowering near Ely
Among fowlers, among fishermen & fogs – & bogs –

Famously her pilgrim's staff took root
& that was Etheldreda's Stow.
They say in Etheldreda's Stow today, they *say* —

That water bubbling from her temporary grave
Was Audrey's Spring: & any bauble
There that's worn around the neck's called tawdry.

  ii

Margery Kempe from Lynn
Would howl and wail "full plenteously"
When told of mirth & pleasures

"Full boisterously" she sobbed
Who was no Wycliffite or Lollard but
Could censure equally

Some bumpkin local reprobate or mighty
Philip Repington and
Greater Arundel upon his Bishop's throne.

Full plenteously, full boisterously
She'd wail: full homely, too!
She was her own Salvation Army band

And drummed and trumpeted vulgarity that
Such as Chesterton would
Understand to be an efficacious pastorale.

Some amanuensis took it down, our first
Biography — be glad! *She* was:
Of plenteous continual weeping by a creature

Who would be the bride of Christ, a pilgrim pure
And not the failed brewer, failed
Miller married to the borough chamberlain

John Kempe that she, said citizens of Lynn,
Pretty clearly was. Contentious;
Weird; she sailed away. The Mamelukes

And Saracens were less impressed with her
Outside the Holy Sepulchre
Than those who'd suffered her for weeks

On board the ship. Said one: a vexèd spirit.
Another: that she'd surfeited on wine.
A third that surely fatal illnesses came on

Like that: *O put her in a heavy sea*
O put her in a little boat
Without a bottom O. Thus, Amanuensis says,

Had each his thoughts. At
York, at Cawood Palace, the Archbishop:
"Woman! – Why, why

Then weepest thou?" And Margery: *Sir, ye*
Shall wish some day
That ye had wept as sore as I!

Dunwich: Winter Visit Alone
— *for Diana*

> *"There is presence in what is*
> *missing; there is history in*
> *there being so little . . ."*

— HENRY JAMES

Young & younger, we were married here
Where cliffs fall into the sea
And most of the village has
Disappeared, drowning in its leas.
I have not loved you less for that.

And if it is chastening to know
That fishermen catch
Their nets on the bell-towers,
Sunken and singing,
I have not loved you less for that,

Even though I have not loved you
As I might have, if, merchant
Or seaman, I had come here with you
To a safe coast in a good time.
No, I have not loved you less for that.

And knowing well the presences here
From the start, and of absence,
Of history alive, still, in so little,
We face the tides and erosions.
And I will not love you less for that.

No, I will not love you less for that.

Verrucas

The solemn doctor, eyeing painfully
My six verrucas,
Closed the heavy office door —

Well, he said, *we often find in fact*
The skinman doesn't
Do much good, his acids

And his sparks, they
All come back — these warts —
And so we usually

Suggest — and you Americans
Are shocked —
(He looked behind him then)

The local witch. The what?
That's right, he said.
I drove a mile or two and found

Her house. A white witch, certainly,
She smiled a kindly smile
& smoked a caked & gnarled briar pipe.

She counted up verrucas, multiplied,
And tied her knots
In just as many strings

As she would bury, burn, or bless.
I used to use a hunk
Of steak for skin disease, she said,

The method's good. I'd slap
It on a warty cheek or sole, and that
Was that. But what with

Meat so dear and all — you'll understand
We don't use mince! this hex'll
Work for you, all right. Three days!

She packed me hobbling off
& said a spell. I tossed a silver coin
In the bottom of her well.

After the Death of Chekhov
– *for Bob Hass*

Anton Pavlovitch has died
At Badenweiler, a spa
Where doctors had sent him,

A doctor, with his beautiful Olga.
They ship the body to Moscow
Where both of us wait at the station.

This is the difference between us:
You, with Chaliapin & Gorki,
Calm the disorderly crowd

And stick with your man: You
Go off in the proper direction
And weep at the grave of the poet,

While I get confused,
Follow a band of the Tzar's
Which is playing a march

In the cortège of a general
Killed in the Japanese War.
Or, when the two coffins arrive

At the platform together,
One in a car labelled
Oysters, and you understand in

A flash which one is Chekhov's,
This is the difference between us:
You return to your wife and honor

The dead by telling hilarious jokes
About Chaliapin & Gorki, while I am sent
To a spa in the car labelled *Oysters*.

You Measure John
(for Diana, at work in the Fitzwilliam)

For posterity you measure John.
For the catalogue
you measure with a tape
his works
and recognize yourself as woman
among women
in the life of this man John, his death.

You measure for the catalogue
the pictures
and their frames
thinking of the others
measuring his need
measuring his pride (who could not
please himself)
measuring his gypsy caravans of children
as he went away to paint, badly,
the famous and the rich.

No, you do not like Augustus John.
Measuring the thickness
of a new biography you offer me
I think –
not. You tell it simply
and with no embellishments yourself.
It is an old story:
some man damages the lives of women
who would love him.
There are various excuses.
One is art.

Mark Twain in the Fens

i

Not the trip of 1872
when fame first fanned an Anglophilia
and glory burst from every side
upon him –
And not the trip of 1879
when he howled for *real coffee,*
corn bread, good roast beef
with taste to it.

The last trip; the exile & the debts.

Thish-yer Smiley had a yeller
one-eyed cow that didn't have no tail . . .
At Brandon Creek, Ship Inn.
They bring him real coffee, good
roast beef with taste to it.

ii

       Recently got up
by him as Joan of Arc,
his eldest daughter once had fled
the Bryn Mawr auditorium –
meningitis all but creeping
up her spine –

He told them all a tingler,
having sworn to her he wouldn't,
called *The Golden Arm.*

     Death made real by hers?
and deathless tales
a part of blame? *My fault, my fault* –
And this: *I'll pay*

though still he dreams each night
about his miracle-working
machine, the Paige Typesetter,
his Dark Angel of print.

iii

Thish-yer Smiley had a yeller
one-eyed cow that didn't have no tail . . .

No one writes it down
or sets it up in type. It is the last
he is going to tell.

It is all over with him. It's
begun. All night long
he tells and tells and tells.

Paul Verlaine in Lincolnshire

i

For a while he had that famous friendship.
But what's inspired debauchery
and manic vision
to illuminations from the English hymnal?
Keble's stanzas? Wesley's? Stanzas
by good Bishop Ken?
Ô mon Dieu, vous m'avez blessé d'amour.

For indulgence, there was Tennyson.
He walked to Boston from the grammar school
in Stickney to confess.

ii

And wrote *Sagesse* there in Lincolnshire.
And went to chapel,
and taught the ugly boys finesse.
He had been condemned to death,
he boasted, in the Siege
of Paris . . .
          Colonel Grantham and
the credulous headmaster
listened to the story
of his clever rescue by Thiers . . .

Even in the hands of Debussy, Fauré,
the catholic lied Verlainian would sing
the strangest nonconformist airs.

Ô mon Dieu, vous m'avez blessé d'amour.

And to proper Mallarmé he wrote
about the absinthe: *I'd still take it
with sugar* . . .
The school record books
do not suggest
that he excelled at rugger.

O there were many rhymes –
But he was on his best behavior,
pious, calm, bourgeois.
The peaceful English countryside
acted on his conscience
like a rudder.

Ô mon Dieu, vous m'avez blessé d'amour.

Mostly Joan Poulson's Recipes Etc.

Thomas Nashe, from Lowestoft,
opined: *a red herring*
is wholesome on a frosty morning

and nowhere are they better cured
than at Yarmouth
and a broiled one is good

for rheumatism, too. Horatio Nelson
hung from a rope
and gathered in the luscious pears all

dangling fruity in the master's little garden
in North Walsham. He found
them exquisitely ripe and to his taste.

Defoe, however, thought
the Suffolk cheese "the worst in England".
Boudicca and Cymbeline

gorged in Colchester on oysters.
Norfolk turkeys
marched in droves through Suffolk villages

and on to London: they took the
18th century to town.
I don't know what Tom Paine liked:

they fed him Thetford porridge.
And Laurence Washington, George's great
great granddad

liked the Meldon new potatoes
with his mutton –
and in Heacham Pocahontas asked John Rolfe

for corn: *which she did not get.*
What I like is Ipswich Almond Pudding,
Aldeburgh Sprats or

Southend Cockle Cakes.
Diana serves up Greengage Mould
and says: *it's good!*

Laura asks for Royston Cakes
but eats a crusty Southwold Dumpling.
Cynouai who'd have a stately

Hen-on-Nest gets potted shrimps
and frowns
but eats them anyway.

Yesterday we had Saxmundham Fourses Cake,
the day before a Damson
Pickle with our Epping Sausages.

There was a time they had here absolutely
nothing & made nettle soup
or tried to eat the earth itself, or stones.

After lunch we walk: past the moated
grange in Parham which was
once the grand estate of first the Uffords

and then the Willoughby d'Ersbys.
We pass dun cows
which still produce the Suffolk cheese

which we enjoy and which
Defoe did not.
And for our tea we eat a Yarmouth herring.

Lines for the Gentlemen

i

1667. And on Landguard beach, 1000 Dutch.
That was the last invasion.
Afterwards, 1753–66,
Governor Thicknesse, thank you, defending, sir.
(And plenty of out-of-work sailors)

ii

And as with piracy, there's honour in it.
And not just honour among thieves –
A rising class will not, they'd tell you,
be put down. Custom?
                                    Brandy! tea, wool, rum,
just name it –
So the word gets round. Someone's
had the pox, someone's
had the plague. All's free trade
at certain cottages where rumored illnesses
or rumored ghosts
keep all but customers away –

Laces for a lady; letters for a spy
And watch the wall, my darling, while the
            Gentlemen go by.

iii

This one watched the wall; that one
closed his eyes.
The headless gunner walked on the embankment.

A crescent moon rose smartly from behind
the nasty gibbet. There are
voices in the back room of The Crown –

and Mr Plumer, MP from Appleby,
speaking in the House
and saying ALL IMPROVEMENT OF THE LAND

HAS BEEN SUSPENDED
while the Parson whispers to his wife
the wages of gin

for our duties
and hides the three enormous tubs
beneath the altar cloth.

4,000,000 gallons of booze are flowing
into England! (Three slow
cutters chasing one fast swipe.)

The publican
has put the spotsmen all to sleep.
Bright lights are flashing

Down the Orwell and the Alde.

More Lines for the Gentlemen
(for L. M., age 6)

i

Thicknesse summons from obscurity
the young Gainsborough

to his Landguard Fort –
The Future's in their hands!

Like muddy Primaveras, there emerge
from busy tidal harbor into history, apotheosis:

Chesterfield and Mrs Siddons
Pitt & Burke & Clive –

Also, though not on anybody's canvas,
not on anybody's list of invitations,

John Pixley Thomas Fidget Black George
Nichols poor Will Laud

& all
the merry rest of them –

smugglers

ii

The Rev. Richard Cobbold, Rector of Wortham & Rural Dean,
writes of Margaret Catchpole's early days:

*Who has not seen the healthy face of childhood in those ever interesting
years when activity commences? And what philanthropist, delighting in
scenes of genuine simplicity and nature, could fail to admire the ruddy
glow of youth, and the elastic step of confidence, with which the young
female peasant bounds to meet a parent or a brother at the welcome hour of
noon. . . .*

My youngest female child, genuinely simple,
ruddy in the glow of youth,
elastic of step, confident, bounding to meet

her male parent at the welcome hour of noon,
gets it wrong. She tells her friend,
bounding with philanthropic step behind her:

My dad's writing a book about snuggling.

    iii

FAMOUS SNUGGLERS OF THE SUFFOLK COAST

On Harwich: Mr Arnott, Master of Rivers: "It was even
considered dangerous to sail across the harbour after dark for
fear of being set upon by snugglers."

From A Visit to Dalmatia

i

Korčula is oleander, cypresses & twisted
fig trees; Korčula is stones –
Lemon trees and stones. Quick mirages
above the stones & olive groves:
Shaky vineyard walls of broken stones and

Stones that must be gathered, piled up
before the shallow arbor roots will
take a tenuous hold
in sandy earth: And shallow stony graves
for Partisan or priest, invader.

Limestone & limestone rock in hills
around Lumbarda, limeface of Sveti Ilija
after Orebić:
                    Rockslides and
washed out roads, karst –
a landscape that will break you on its back
or make a sculptor of you –

Lozica, Kršinić, Ivan Jurjević-Knez.

ii

Or if not a sculptor then a fisherman.
Or, it would have once.
                    Looking at the empty streets
at noon, Toni Bernidić
tells me it's the woist and hottest
day so far in June – he learned
his English in Brooklyn
during the war –
But his house is cool, and so
are the wines: Grk, Pošip, Dingač. . . .

He tells me of the wooden ships
he built, each one taking
him a year: but well made, well made –
The work, he says,
was heavy – pointing to his tools.

Now he has no work: the island's
income is from tourists
and the flushed young men who'd once
have been apprentices
sport their *Atlas* badges, ride their
scooters to the Park or Marco Polo
or the Bon Repos
and show their muscles to the breezy
blue-eyed girls
whose wealthy fathers order loudly
wiener schnitzel

wienerschnitzel and stones.

Friendship

One day I do you a good turn. Then
You do me *two* good turns.
I am pleased by that & say so the next day.

You break the lead in your pencil.
I loan you mine.
You give me an expensive fountain pen.

I play you a recording of The Modern Jazz Quartet.
Though you like Milt Jackson's vibes, you
Take me to *The Ring* at Covent Garden after which

We introduce each other to our wives.
My wife teaches your wife how to cook fondues.
Your wife teaches my wife how to live.

I dedicate my book to you & you are moved.
You make a character of me in yours:
It is singled out for praise by the reviewers.

I give my mistress to your loyalest disciple.
Claiming he is bored with her, you have
The wench returned; her skills are much improved.

When I sing my secret lute song about mountains,
You take me to the mountains
In your car: You have a cabin there

Where after drinks we agree to a primitive contest.
Preparing for it, you
Scar your face grotesquely with a razor blade.

Upon return, I burn for you my manuscript.
For me you smash your files. I wreck my mother's house.
You wreck your only daughter's mind.

In the end, I write a letter saying:
I forgive you. But you do not write back.
It is now the time for silence.

For we are friends. We love each other very much.

Agape
(after the poem by César Vallejo)

I won't say anyone comes here and asks.
They haven't this afternoon
Asked me for anything much. Nothing!

Not one leper presented himself.
I haven't today
Kissed my quota of sores.

In so fine a parading of lights, I haven't
Seen a single burial flower.
Lord, Lord: I've died so little today,

I'm sorry, forgive me. Everybody goes by
But nobody asks for a thing.
Mal, mal in my hands, like a *cosa ajena.*

If you've mislaid it it's here!
Well, I've gone to the door & I've shouted.
How many doors get slammed in my face!

Something *ajeno ajeno* roots in my soul
And I don't tell you somebody comes here & asks.
Lord, Lord: I've died so little today.

Brandon, Breckland: The Flint Knappers
(after a chapter in Julian Tennyson's Suffolk Scene*)*

The Forestry Commission was about to plant
the Breckland on the day young Julian Tennyson

visited the Edwardses, last knappers of Brandon.
Because some tribes in Central Africa

hadn't heard about percussion caps
there still was business for the craftsmen

that supplied the flints for Wellington
and watched the plovers & the curlews dip at home.

Alien, the Breckland seemed as sinister & desolate
to Tennyson as 1938, the stark flint cottages

all shining darkly in reflecting pools
of stone and dusty sorrel, riding in the ragwort

and the bugloss, or jutting out of bracken,
heather, thin brown grass.

Wheatears, stonechats, whinchats, pipits –
all in the same still air –

and Julian, once a Suffolk countryman's Huck Finn,
feeling terrors coming on him

now at twenty-three, feeling *loosed in some
primeval, flat and limitless arena –*

leagues and leagues and leagues of it, he wrote,
severed from the rest of England.

Brandon on the Little Ouse was a relief from that,
though still in Breckland.

Malting, watermeadows, fine old bridge –
as lovely a corner as any I have found in Suffolk.

The elder Edwards, coughing, takes him
in his workshop, shuts the door, and points:

topstone, wallstone, floorstone chips
from Lingheath Common quarry, ornaments & tinders,

flints for muskets, carbines, pistols –
quartered first, then flaked and knapped with

pointed hammer on a flattened rod of iron.
When the headmen learn about percussion caps

the show's all over, Edwards said.
And anyway we've not got one apprentice

and the quarrier's retired. It would die with him,
his art, these mysteries of Breckland.

Meanwhile Tennyson looks on amazed
as Edwards bevels edges, hammers, hammers, talks:

I did it on the radio into a microphone, I
did it on the BBC before the news.

There are reports. Off in Central Africa
sprawls a man who feels of a sudden loosed in some

primeval flat and limitless arena –
leagues and leagues and leagues of it, he thinks

in his delirium. There is a flight of birds.
On Berner's green: an Air Ministry bombing-ground;

Here the Forestry Commission will plant firs.
Badgers and foxes, jays and crows

will populate the land the curlews flee, *and when*
the Old Guard fell before great Wellington

England sang the knappers of the Brandon flints!
It is the year of Munich. Tennyson will die

in Burma from a piece of shrapnel the size of any
smallish hag-stone he'd have found

among discarded chips on Edwards' dusty floor
and which his copy of George Borrow

pressing pages from a manuscript of *In Memoriam*
will not deflect. Reflected in his book,

an Indian summer. Ice will one day lift
the Blaxhall Stone itself as far as Brandon moor.

59 Lines Assembled Quickly
Sitting on a Wall Near the Reconstruction
of the Lady Juliana's Cell

Heavily   heavily
hidden away –

the door is
barred & barred   and

singing
veni creator

spiritus   "a service
of Enclosure"

& the cell
is consecrated

and the door
is barred   and

singing
veni creator

spiritus you have
a window on

the church you have
a window on

the world
and appearances

and revel-
ations   visions!

"showings"
to a soul *that*

cowde
no letter: cowde —

could, cloud
no cloud or cold

unknowing sin
is what

there loud? or
quiet sin is what

behoved? or is
behovable

il convient que
le péché

existe: le péché is
serviceable

what is
an anchorhold what is

an anchoress
the Lady Juliana's

one re-
corded visit from the

frenzied Margerie Kempe
as praise

& praise & gesture
I prefer

to Juliana's
Kemp's

the *other* Kemp's
Will Kemp's

who morris danced
from London

days   on days
from London

Kemp's who
lept!   immortally

this Norwich wall

26 June 1381/1977

i: North Walsham: The Fields

And he, Despenser, tried to keep hold
Of the dyer's head

As the crowd of them, gawkers
& priests, tinkers & tailors & wastrels

(Gentry too, thinking already: *reredos!*
A gift for him, a

Presentiment) lurched along
With the horsecart off to the place

Of undoing, Lidster's undoing who'd heard –
Who'd heard of *The Kynges*

Son who'd paye for al,
The mullere who'd ygrounde smal – but

Was paying himself,
Tied by a foot with the same rope

That they'd hang him with, after
The drawing. And he

Henry Despenser, the Bishop "Lespenser" –
miles amatus, boni pastoris mens,

For so it says on his brass –
Hopping behind the cart like a toad,

The cart they dragged the dyer behind
For that was the law:

To be dragged to the place of undoing.
This, however, was extra:

The Bishop himself coddling your head
In his skirts

And you "The King of the Commons",
"The Idol of Norfolk"

Whose bell had been rung
By Ball and Tyler and Straw. Oh

This dispenser of justice was special,
sui generis the man who

Had caught you, tried you, confessed you,
The man who would hang you

See you in quarters, one for each of
The earth's: hopping

Behind the cart like a toad . . .
And reaching out for your head   which

Aoi!   he'd drop on a cobble a cobble
a cobble and *there*

Then catch it up again, mother it back
In his apron, your head

Like an apple or melon or globe. Where,
Where did you travel, where

Did you think you could go –
The two of you, then, staff, of one, life?

ii: St Luke's Chapel, Norwich Cathedral

We look at the reredos, the retables.
Of course the "subject"

Is "Christ" . . . But the blood & the power
That steadied the hand

And shook the knees and the wits of the
Master from Norwich – *that*

Was the blood and the power of Dyer
And Bishop, of Lidster

And Henry Despenser. Behind me somebody
Mumbles the word *chiliastic*.

His fellow-tourist says, looking hard: it's
Absolutely fantastic!

The five panels escaped the smashings
Of Cromwell. The five

Scenes from the Passion here are restored.
And we may embrace

The arcana, study
The photomicrographic specifics:

A patient lady explains: *malachite*,
Azurite: And the head of Christ is restored!

The rotten wood is restored: the order
Is restored. *Israelite*,

Trotskyite. Edmund Burke said of the famous
Rhyme: *it rhymes!* And also: *a sapient*

Maxim: When Adam delved and Eve span, who
Was then the gentle man?

Nobody knows what Lidster said, but that's
What he heard: *The Kynges son schal*

Paye for al
The mullere hath ygrounde smal – and

Paid it himself,
Tied by a foot with the same rope

They'd etcetera. *Spin*:
The painting and the restoration

Are brilliantly done. *Delve*: the revolt
Alas was untimely – even Engels

Would say so – and Henry Despenser's work
Was brilliantly done –

And us with our heads still on our necks?
With books in our laps,

Stupid or giddy, gawking –
Us with the eyes still in their sockets

And tongues still in our mouths –
Where do we travel, where

Do we think we can go –
All of us, now, staff, of one, life?

On the Death of Benjamin Britten

Operas! A feast for burghers, said Adorno.
And of your work: The apotheosis
Of meagerness, a kind of fast. That's
A cruel case against you
And it may have weight, in time.
But let's call meagerness
Economy today
And call the bourgeoisie the people
Who like me have (barely) what it costs
To listen and who like to hear
These songs, but who will pay a price.
Economies of living soon enough
Make meager even music of the spheres!
To be of use, you said.
Directly and deliberately I write
For human beings. And not
Posterity — for which the general outlook
Isn't very bright.

A tenor mourns. And you lie down in Aldeburgh
One last time. But you have work to do
In spite of what the two of us have said.
A tenor sings. When you
Get out there over the horizon
This December morning with the likes
Of Peter Grimes
Row your shining boat ashore
And be extravagant in song:
Leave economy to the ungrateful living
Who will need it, whose Justice
And whose History have multiplied unendingly
Expenses by Apotheoses by Sublimes.

III The Stefan Batory
and Mihail Lermontov Poems

Being, among other things, a comic lament for the decade of the
1960s, and a private celebration, both early and late, of the
American Bicentennial and the Queen's Silver Jubilee.

for Cynouai and Laura

The Stefan Batory Poems

One: Hacheston, Suffolk

To begin with a name –
Katarsky –
          To begin
to leave with a name, Polish,
for a Polish ship named
for another, for Stefan Batory.
          Name of Katarsky.
Name of Stefan Batory.

To begin to leave this place
I've lived that's no more
mine than his, Katarsky's,
a village near his farm,
a land that's rich with legends
not my own, not his.

Name of Katarsky. Names
of his twins, Andrzej & Zbyszek.
Slid down haystacks with
my wife, these twins, when
she was five.
          Andrzej & Zbyszek.
Katarsky.
          After the war
when hay grew again
into haystacks, when the Poles
in England, some of them,
went home . . .

Katarsky, says the lady in
the shop Oh Well Katarsky sir
I'll tell you what I know
about Katarsky and that farm
and how he might as well have

gone on home the Russians *or*
the Germans and I
have to interrupt, say

                    no, oh stop it now

I only wanted
a Polish name for a poem:
only wanted a way to say goodbye.

Two

I wake up having dreamed of whales
To find my family sleeping in
Their berths. The breakfast menu
Is under the door: delicious
Smells in the passageway . . .

I can have Soki, Zupy Sniadaniowe, Jajka, Omlety, Ryby,
something from the Zimny Bufet, Przetwory Owocowe on my
bread, Sery, a hot cup of Kawa bez kofeiny (coffeinevrije:
decaffeinated). Or mint tea and compôte. The day's program
includes Holy Mass in the Cinema, a matinée concert of
chamber music (Vivaldi, Handel, and Telemann), afternoon
tea, an American film with dubbed-in Polish, cocktails, bingo
and dancing. Wife nor daughters stir. I open Mickiewicz. . . .

"Ye comrades of the Grand Dukes of Lithuania, trees of
Bialowieza, Switez, Ponary, and Kuszelewo! whose shade once
fell upon the crowned heads of the dread Witenes and the great
Mindowe, and of Giedymin, when on the height of Ponary, by
the huntsmen's fire, he lay on a bear skin, listening to the song of
the wise Lizdejko; and, lulled by the sight of the Wilia and the
murmur of the Wilejko, he dreamed of the iron wolf. . . ."
What an invocation! Comrades and trees! The trees are
important.

Last night as we passed Land's End I spoke for hours with a
couple from Newcastle leaving England to emigrate to
Canada. They stared hard, saying goodbye, looking into the
darkness for a last flickering English light. They're sorry to leave
but can't, so they told me, save a sixpence in a year. I wished
them luck in Canada. And comrades. And trees.

I decide to go on deck.

Three

You, Batory, an *elected* monarch.
You owed it all to Henry de Valois.
Lithuania backed the Russian Tzar,
The Church took the Archduke; the
Anti-German *szlachta* was for any
Anti-German. You from Transylvania.
But leave it to the French:
Ambassadorially, the Bishop of
Valance distributes rings to
Get the throne for edgy de Valois.
Who took one look and fled:
Brother Charles croaked
And he (Valois) was Henry Three
Sipping port in Paris.
The horsy gentry blinked and summoned –
Married you to Royal Anne Jagiellon.

How much did you know? Not as much
As Canon Koppernigk who made
His measurements at Frauenburg (which
He called Gynopolis) pretending in
His *Revolutions* that he stargazed
On the Vistula away from battlefields
And Teutonic Knights. Not as much
As Koppernigk whose system, Prince,
Because he longed for Cracow
And his youth, would run your ship
If not your ship of state aground,
But this at least: How to maintain
Access to the sea; how to use
A chancellor's advice. And how
With Danzig yours to drive with
Peasant infantries the Russian Bear
Beyond Livonia to the Pope.

The cavalry was not deployed –
Horses in their stables, and at hay.

Four

A day passes, the weather is rough. We meet Poles, Englishmen, Irish, Americans, Czechs, Swiss, Frenchmen, Germans, Russians, and two Japanese. Diana teaches Laura how to approach a new friend: *Was ist Ihre Name, bitte? Was ist Ihre Name?* It turns out to be Alma. Laura is delighted. Cynouai is seasick and goes early to bed. It's my night for the movies.

The Cinema is down a flight of stairs outside the dining room – and *down, low,* so very low in the ship the room should be some kind of hold or place for ballast. In the middle of *Little Big Man*, I realize with a start that I am actually under water. If we spring a leak, this theatre will instantly fill like a tank, the watertight door will be closed by a panicky steward, and there we'll be – each of us holding his nose and floating to the ceiling as Dustin Hoffman shrieks in Polish and tomahawks fall from the sky. . . .

Was ist Ihre Name, bitte?

Was ist Ihre Name?

Five: The Library

i

The weather improves. Serious now,
I attend to correspondence.
Here they read the news and study
Not Mickiewicz or the other unread
Poets on these shelves
But ups and downs of stocks
And the extraordinary language
Of my President reported in the
Daily Polish/English mimeo gazette.
The banalities and rhetoric of power
Dovetail with the mathematics
Of the market: Soon the brokers,
As in 1929, will sail nicely
From the upper stories
Of the highest buildings in New York,
Their sons will pluck the feathers
From their hair and look for jobs
A thousand miles from the ethnic
Bonfires of their dreams, the
Poor will stand in bread lines,
And I, a curio from 1959, will find
My clientele reduced to nuns
And priestly neophytes. I return
To Indiana – the only place
Save Utah where the Sixties,
Though Peter Michelson was waiting,
Failed to arrive.

ii

I am, as Peter thought I would be,
Going back. But slowly.
The journey takes nine days.
Unanswered letters – his and Ernie's,

Kevin's, Mrs. Harris's –
They weigh on me.
My friends, my gifted student,
My daughters' much beloved nurse.

"Too much mopin' now," says P.,
"And many mumblin's . . .
                                    But you *will*
Be coming back because although
You think yourself no gringo, John,
You are: and this is where
The gringo fighting is.
Or gringo baiting.
Or: whatever the conditions will allow.
I'll expect you here in August."

And Kevin writes: "I'm scared
Of everything and wholly lack
Direction . . .
                        Plus, of course,
I'm personally responsible
For all of human misery: the
Shoeless Appalachians, every
Starving Indian. And what
I like to do is eat, talk to
Charming educated people, drink
Good wine, read the best
Pornography, discuss at leisure
Every new advance
In Western decadence."

E. has written to me once a year for eight years
straight. This year it's about my poems. And his. His muse
grows younger (he is over sixty-five) as mine begins to age. My
attraction to quotation, commentary, pastiche: exhaustion? or
the very method of abstention that he recommends? Many days
I'd be a scribe, a monk – and I, like monk and scribe, am
permitted to append the meanings that my authors may have

missed. "He abandoned himself to the absolute sincerity of pastiche": on Ekelöf, Printz-Påhlson. Otherwise? Poets know too much. We bring things on us. There is always an extra place at the table: the poem, as Ernie says, arranges it . . .

With total serenity ·
He abandoned pastiche for patchouli
For patchouli and panache
He abandoned his panto-panjandrum
With utter contempt for panache
He abandoned patchouli
He abandoned himself with unspeakable simplicity
To Pastrami.

Inventions organized to dance
A variation of our lives?
Or simply evidence?
Or letters to and from our friends?
Here, the doctor said, is your scarab.
Prospero whispers in one ear
And Lenin in the other.

Six

Familiar, the dull rattle
and buzz of screws
abates; we glide. . . .

A hundred yards away
Gothic dips and spires –
St Brendan's "floating crystal castle."

Calving from some ancient
ice sheet, pinnacles around a central
mass like sails,

it makes good time: radar brought
back only sea return – echoes from the waves.
A spotlight caught it in the fog.

Late, late . . .
Are we in Brendan's time?
We suffer sea return.

The ship will tilt on its keel,
roll on the last wave
over the edge of the earth.

Seven

The Batory, a passenger says, once belonged to the Holland-American line; it was, indeed, the famous "Student Ship." If this is true, my strange sense of *déjà vu* is explained by more than the simple fact of my being, after sixteen years, at sea again. Can it be, in fact, that I am on the "Student Ship" once more? which flies the colors now of Poland?

Every detail has seemed so extraordinarily familiar: the location of rooms, the structure of the decks (did I kiss that girl from Georgia *there*, just *there*?), the clever organization of space which makes what is tight and constraining appear to be comfortable and larger than it is. The same ship! I was on my way, eventually, to Turkey, where I thought to save my small-town childhood love from becoming an adult. She had spent a year in Istanbul with her parents; her letters had grown sophisticated and knowing; I was afraid. Seventeen and virginal, I sailed from New York thinking I was Henry James and clutching to my heart every available illusion about myself and the world.

Ghosting on the bridge or in the engine room, hailing Flying Dutchmen or staring darkly at the sea, any foolish sentimental shade aboard is mine.

Eight

Two violins, a double-bass,
Drums, piano, and trumpet –
Accordion, of course:
A curious sound.
For our tea they play us schmaltz
And polkas.

At night, the same musicians
Are transformed: they make
A fearful frantic jazz-cum-rock
With other instruments
And sing a polyphonic polyglot
Appropriate to
Mid-Atlantic revels.

On a sleeve, four gold rings of lace, an anchor above; on
another, three gold rings. I point out the captain and his second
officer at an adjacent table. Cynouai: "Then who's driving the
boat?" Laura: "It drives itself."

Over cakes, I polish my translation from the sixteenth
century Polish of the famous Jewish Cossack, Konrad Konrad.
He is not, unlike Michelson, Matthias and Sandeen, altogether
serious in his treatment of the terrifying retribution falling upon
the unfortunate bard as a reward for the practice of his craft.
Thus I render the piece for a vanished upper-upper British
accent and into an idiom which I think would not displease, say,
Edward Lear.

Nine

Edgar Allan Poe
Wanted to go
To Poland.
So, probably, did Lafayette.
In 1830 he was too old.
James Fenimore Cooper
Cried: "Brothers!"
Everyone remembered Kosciuszko.
In Paris, Mickiewicz
Was eloquent: "The West,"
He said, "It dies of its doctrines!"
With Michelet and Quinet,
They cast him in bronze.
Of Lamennais: "He weeps for me."
Of Napoleon: "Come!"

Divination by Jacksonian Hickory:
Buchanan liked his ambassadorship,
His high teas with the Tzar.
In spite of Samuel Morse, that
Established Gomulka.
Churchill said: "It's no
Time for quarrels . . ."
Sikorsky crashed in his plane.
"Hel falls," said Hemar.
"Assassins steal our Westerplatte."

Batory, they've thrown your best
Philosopher out of Warsaw.
The one who stenographically took
The Devil's report.
I don't think Rosa Luxemburg
Would be pleased. She,
Like you, was a fighter & proud.

I like to think of Rilke's Angels
And his loving explanations to von Hulewicz.
I don't think about Esterhazy
Or Chopin. I think of Hass's poem
For his Polish friends in Buffalo.
Hass – who reads Mickiewicz
For his mushrooms.

I think of Jean Rousseau: "At least
Do not allow them to digest you!"
I think of Kazimierz Stanislaw Gzowski –
Knighted by Victoria, founder
Of the city of Toronto.
I think of Materski in the forests
Of my native Ohio: "Send no
Exiles inland." Ohio – unaware
Of 1830, of 1848.

Calling for my gambling debts,
The learned Purser
Quotes for me a famous
Unacknowledged source in Yiddish:
"Oh, frayg nit: 'Vus iz it?'
Los mir gehn zu machen Visit."

We approach the Gulf of St Lawrence.

Ten

The long aerial of Alma's German radio brings in, at last, the news. The C.B.C. is pleased: Nixon quits. That man named Gerald Ford is president. "An honest Nixon," someone says. "A sort of Hoover type." A little late, I think, for Hoover now. But we are on the river, the sun will surely rise, and very few are interested in politics. An age of boredom dawns. New Poland steams toward Old Quebec.

I gather friends around me in
The eerie morning haze:
" 'Sea hunger,' " I say, " 'has gripped
The West. It will hack its way
To the Atlantic.' Friends,
I'd have rather written that
Than take the town. There died Wolfe
Victorious. 'Let us build,' said
Eisenhower, 'a canal!'

"*Franciscus Primus*,
Dei Gratia Francorum Rex.
What, bearing such
A cross, did Cartier observe?"

Indians, I suppose. Exotic birds. Looking for Cathay, he didn't hear, his German aerial extended to its length, such twitterings as these: 'I want to talk with you about what kind of line to take: I now want Kleindienst on it – It isn't a matter of trust. You have clearly understood that you will call him, give him the directions. I don't want to go off now to get us: ah! To maken ani deeeeeeeeals.'

Indians. And exotic brids. At sea there is no time, and therefore do ye joke about solemnities. Therefore do ye sip Courvoisier or ponderously lie, or sleep with other people's wives. But on a river? On a waterway that Eisenhower built? *Was ist Ihre Name*, after all? Open your Mickiewicz. Abandon

your panjandrum. Suffer, when the hum of screws abates, your
sea return.

On one arrival here the crew abandoned ship: engineers
and deck hands diving through the portholes, swimming
toward the haunted isle of Parkman's Marguerite. Thevet the
cosmographer at Natron heard *her* tale. Polish seamen didn't.
Instead of *Little Big Man*, Warsaw played *Dziady* on a Forefather's
Eve. George Sand had found it stronger stuff than *Faust*.
Gomulka sent his tanks against the Czechs.

Am I guilty of obscure
Complicities, America? O Poland?
The ugly birthright of
My sinking class? Western
Nations dress themselves
To dream a dull apocalypse
While I float down that
River loved by old Champlain
And every last Algonquin
In his long canoe. I'm guilty
And in luck in lousy times.

I walk the promenade deck, look at archipelagos and tiny
fishing villages, return Mickiewicz to his shelf between the
propaganda and the porn. I slip my bookmark, Jessie's letter
dated just about a year ago, into a jacket pocket. Then I take it
out and read it once again. "These few lines," she says, "to let
you hear from me. I am up but I am havin trouble with my arm
an shoulder pains me like before. But I was glad to hear from
you an I am glad you all are well. I thought about you all
because you did say you was

Comin over before leavin an I
Didn't know what happen. I don't

Know whats wrong with people now an
I'm afraid to set out on the porch

Any more. Give my love to the girls
An write me again some time. This

Will be all for now. It's real
Cold here. Love from your friend,

Jessie Harris."

The Mihail Lermontov Poems

Dogeared Proem: in which I decide to change my name before returning to England on a Russian ship after two years of sincerely trying to come to terms with America

Once I had a Polish friend, Zymierski.
He changed his name to Zane.
Dane Zane it became. (It's Zane Grey I blame.)
Perhaps you've seen his ivory-handled cane
In the historical museum
In Barcelona, Spain.
I resolved, in disapproval,
Never to change my name –
Even for the best of reasons,
Even in the worst of times,
Even for the sake of love, the sake of fame.

Still, today I've heard it claimed
The Baltic Shipping Company's
Investigating all the old Decembrists.
Safety first, I say.
Anyway, like Pushkin,
I'm interested in my maternal side.
(My father's fathers I cannot abide.)
No curly hair, no swarthy
Abyssinian face, I can't embrace
An Ibrahim (Great Peter's Black,
In lace); nor, like his
Successor Lermontov, find
My line extends to Ercildoune
And gnomic Thomas with his elves.
But I can reach for names
That suit me just the same.

Like old Arzeno, watchmaker
And jeweler, born in some Italian drain,
Republican and Methodist
(Rare, as the obituary read,
For one of his nativity)
Who, once he reached Ohio
"Enjoyed the largest gains
In all of Georgetown" –
And Kirkpatrick, Scottish-Irish Democratic
Miller who was Abolitionist before
The Civil War, him whose
Moniker my social-working Aunt
Still answers to
In hot unsociable and palmy
Mid-Floridian lanes.
Her Christian handle's Jean,
Not Jane.

Arzeno and Kirkpatrick! How happily
I'd hyphenate your names!
Great grandfathering immigrants
Might summon if combined
In just proportions
A Maternal Spirit
Powerful as any Abyssinian or Elf
To whom I would declaim
A strange refrain:

– "O wild Italian-Irish Lass & Muse
O take aim and snipe at
(If not slay)
The heavy and judicial German
In me called Matthias.
Protect with *sprezzatura*
And some Gaelic gall this voyager
His life
His children and his wife.
O help me put on my disguise.

Help to make me good
And wise.
I'll be to God and man
Jack Arzeno-Kirkpatrick
For an odd span
Of days
Of days and nights."

Two

I'm introduced to the distinguished touring poet. He's a grand sight, all right. I'm mightily impressed. Dark hair, dark complexion, dark and piercing eyes. His companion (from the Secret Police? is our artist on a leash?) remarks with irritation: "Watch him. He will gaze contemptuously at all around him. He will greet you," the companion maintains, "with an unfriendly stare; he will be rude, insolent, and arrogant; he will respond, if he responds at all, to any remark of your own, with a sharp retort." I look at him and say: "You happen in one hidden glorious hour to waken in the longtime silent soul once more mysterious virgin springs of power." He responds with a sharp retort. I say: "Then trust them not? nor let their song be heard? Veil them in dark oblivion once again?" *In measured verse and icy rigorous words: a sharp retort.*

So. We understand one another immediately. With a little quick maneuvering in and around the more exotic midwestern towns we manage to lose his shadow somewhere in the vicinity of French Lick, Indiana. We fall immediately into a discussion of his life and times. "Bad times," he says. "Hard life." "Boring," he says. "Repressive." I smile sympathetically. "Listen," he says. "Nicky the First, after all! The Gendarme of Europe, The Cop. I exist at the will or the whim of a Cop." I smile sympathetically. "Monroe," I reply, "and his Doctrine. It's late applications. Not to mention Tzar Andrew – his powers & pains." He says: "The elegant and Jacobin Spring of December failed when I was young." "Yes," I sigh. "I remember the weather." And he: "The fate of Pushkin." And I: "The fate of Poe." He buys me a Vodka Collins. In my imagination we are transported to Tsarkoie Selo where the poet, Cornet of the Life Guard Hussars, entertains. Saber blades, as Viskovaty has described the scene, "serve as standards for the sugar-heads which, with rum poured over them, burn with a beautiful blue fire, poetically lighting the drawing room from which for the sake of effect all candles have been removed."

"I became famous in a single day," he tells me after a couple of drinks. "Anna Mihailovna Hitrovo – we knew her as *la lèpre de la société* – showed that angry poem of mine to the Tzar. 'Fuel for revolution' she told the greedy crew that round his sceptre crawled. They sent me to the Nijegorodsky Dragoons where I slept in the open fields to the howling of jackals. I ate *churyok*, drank Kakhetian wine, and dressed like a Circassian with a gun in my belt. Still, Bielinsky praised the 'iron clangour' of my mighty line, and the mountains were a consolation." Abruptly, he stops. After a long and awkward silence, he blows out the sweet smelling and eerie blue-burning sugar heads of my imagination. "Do you like the sea?" he enquires. "You'll perish, of course, in a duel."

He heads east in a '73 Datsun. He turns into a ship.

Three

Ah, the stuff of greatness: Lermontov! Lermontov!
And the sources of greatness, Pushkin
And Byron. A lecture on greatness: by Olga
Our cultural commissar. An example
Of greatness, contemporary: our captain, Aram Mihailovich.
A great weight: the 20,000 tons of our ship.
A great mountain range: the Caucasus.
Great is the sauna, the caviar, the vodka
And the Volga: great is the Volga Boatman, the boatman
Himself and the song in his honour.
The bridge is great, the ballroom is great,
The bars are great (and the booze in the bars): also
The bilgewater is great and the bureaus
In the Bureaucracy: great are the drawers
Of each bureau, the pencils and papers inside,
The paper-clips and the pens.
Great is the promenade deck and the number three hatch.
Leningrad is a great city.
Moscow is a great city. The Odessa steps are
Great steps, especially in the film
By Eisenstein, the great Russian director.
A Russian passenger tells me
In the gym: "Our system is greater than yours!"
Great is the gym, the barbells and the jumping ropes:
These will make us strong! The waiter pours
Us at breakfast endless glasses
Of pineapple juice: these will make us strong.
Marx will make us strong. Lenin will make us strong.
Great & strong is the ghost of Engels
Far away in the ruins of Birmingham mills
And great is our chief engineer, Vasily Vasilyevich,
Who runs the engines turning propellers
Made by the great propeller makers of Leningrad.
Great is the Neva River and the drawbridge across it
The Winter Palace the Rostral Column the gate
Of Mihailovsky Garden the Admiralty the Palace Square

And Isaac's Cathedral, all of these sights
To be seen on a tour of the great city of Leningrad.
Great is cyrillic calligraphy
And beautiful too in the hands of ancient scribes
Who lived in ancient abodes before our own glorious times.
Great are our own glorious times
And great are the writers of our own glorious times
Their works and their days. Great is
The writers' union and Ivan Ivanovich its guiding spirit
And great patriotic example:
Great are his works:
Especially great are his volume of poems *Praise*
To The Combine Harvester and his novels
Bazooka and *Love in a Sewage Treatment Facility.*
Great is the port side of the ship
And the starboard, great is the fore and the aft,
Great is the bow and the bowsprit
And the Bow of Rostropovich its resin and hairs:
Great too is Shostakovich, sometimes:
His greatness appalls us in his Leningrad Symphony
If slightly less in his decadent earlier works
And his very private string quartets.
Great without doubt is the Bolshoi Ballet all the time
And great are the fountains
Of Peter the Great who was certainly great
In his time
And in his time a progressive.
Great is my cabin
Cabin 335
Where I read an anthology
Full of English and American poems
In Russian
And find in juxtaposition
One by Kenneth Koch
And one by Stephen Spender
And think continually
And think continually of what is great.

Four

i

And I have broken my resolution to stick it out in America.
I said I'd suffer sea return, abandon my Panjandrum. I made
some very solemn public promises in *TriQuarterly* magazine,
Number 35: Yes, Bielinsky, in the famous *Stefan Batory Poems*,
written on another ship, heading in the opposite direction.
Stern and manly verses, iron clanging, yea! in every line.
Readers world-wide are asking: Did I ever see Mrs. Harris
again? How is Michelson doing? What became of Kevin? Is
Sandeen writing poems? How do I pronounce: Mickiewicz?
Mickiewicz? And who is wise Lizdejko? And who is wise Printz-
Påhlson? Have I been sued for plagiarism? Libel? I didn't, did
I, change my name to Arzeno-Kirkpatrick for nothing.

Dreary, gentle reader, were my days in Indiana;
Drab beyond my dreams. Besides,
My wife is British. She'd abandon me entirely
If I didn't take her to England
For the Bicentennial Year.

Also, I've had troubles with a lovely lady student.
Whose wrath, you see, I flee. "*vi sva-BOD-ni
s'i-VOD'-n'e V'E-chi-rem?*" I asked, though in English. *What?*
"*DAY-t'i mn'e vash A-dr'is.*" *Who?*
("Possession of an innocent, an unfolded soul,"
Says Lermontov's Pechorin: "Boundless delight!")
"Maybe I'm too old for this," I told her in the night.
"Hath delight," she cried, "its bounds and bonds?
"Doth brilliant Abelard just fall to bits in flight?"

"Which bits are falling?" I enquired.

England! Which bits are falling? *What?*
In Dunwich
And in Dunkirk.
What?
Will there always be an England
Now that Wilson's out
Now that there's a drought in Suffolk?
Sings Callaghan, P.M., waking up
At Number Ten to pour
The North Sea Oil on his Kraut:
God bless the god bless the godblessed Yanks.
O help us sell our tanks
To somebody, thanks!

We know the Saudis want the Tower.
Already
Arabs own the Dorchester
And Royal Kens-
Ington Hotels. They hold controlling
Interest in the Cotswolds
And the Fens.
Nigeria is going to want the Inns of Court.
Castles reassemble daily
In our dreams
In dirty streets in Cairo and Uganda.
Better they should grow
On rocky California coasts. Better
Move the Bank of England into Berkeley or Big Sur.
Better ship the Bodleian to Boston or New York.
Who, after all,
Saved the battle field at Hastings? *What?*
Bought the bloomin' battle field for Blighty. *What?*
Better that a worthy bridge
Should span a tract of Arizona desert sands
Than sink into the Thames
Or fall into the hands & vanish in the lands of

Libretto: for E.P.

To Mister K said Mister Nix
I want to see a little symmetry of islands
in the sticks
both east and west of us.
I've got a little fix on certain stars
tells
which island, Baby,
maybe
's gonna be
of States the 51st of 'em
in one
nine seven
six.

Five

I carry with me once again: the mail.
There is, after all, nearly always
Mail to chasten or to cheer – (it reached me
This time in New York) – and there are two
Classes of friends: those who write
When one's away
And those who don't or won't.

Says Joe: "As an added attraction in my dreams last night, there
was a letter from you at the end of which was an addendum in
red ink. The writing was large, spacious, and very lucid. It was
some sort of a note from your wife, but it was signed: "Cissy"
(?). Suddenly the three of us were in an open motorboat cruising
through the Everglades, accompanied by a group of people
called "The Mini-Multi Nations": Each person was dressed
most luridly in his native garb, and each, in turn, sang the
folksongs of his native land in native lingo. There was a German
on board, complete with green Alpine cap and burly legs, on
whom the whole group turned when it came to be his time to
sing. As we proceeded up the river, another, smaller motorboat
crossed our bow. There were two fishermen in it, and one of
them, quite ugly, cast his line into our boat, dragging the
German out of it and into the water. Anyway, I'm writing letters
to graduate schools and wondering: Have I got a chance at
Heidelberg?"

Was muss man tun um ein guter Seeman zu sein.
What to do to be a good sailor.
Wenn Sie sich unwohl fühlen, müssen Sie sich im Ferien in der
frischen Luft bewegen, mit etwas beschäftigen, und wenn
Sie irgend können-etwas essen.
If you feel ill, keep moving and busy in the fresh air; this will
often drive away dizziness and save you the not so good
experience of MAL DE MER.

From an anonymous informant: the news that, in my absence, I have been the victim of a parody and mock-panegyric by a certain (clearly pseudonymous) N. Talarico published in a local (to the bush) but most notorious little mag. I am sent quotations from the choicest bits of his encomium: "To Matthias, as He Makes A Name For Himself." He begins, himself, with a quote: ". . . not unlike Darwin playing the trombone to his French beans." My portrait ("Sir, the subject is mean – like Eustace Budgel who threw himself into the Thames") follows at once: "Weary hair that sprawls like a hanging garden of King Neb's grass, vaulted forehead, wrinkles, fluting, proud dripping eyes, the schizoid clergyman buried under one too many vows . . . nerves frizzing and popping like the ectoskeleton of some prodigious frying crustacean. . . ." But I cannot go on.

Patty writes: "I told McMurphy and McBride I was going to invite you to become a Catholic and they *hooted*. So I won't but still I think it's what we have to offer. Phytophthora root rot infests your pseudopodium. I saw Solzhenitsyn on TV; it was apocalyptic. *I* was apoplectic, afraid for the first time. I have something wrong with a bone in my foot. Stop drooling in self-pity, I tell myself. Face it, this is your home. Why do you keep going away? Think of McMurphy and McBride. I wanted to hide and am hiding but now I want to be found.

Who do you think has a death wish?
Have a good year, boss, truly.
Regards. The end.
Olé.
Patty."

Six

Around and about. With the girls, first,
For haircuts. Less is more, as someone said,
And Cynouai looks ravishing
And two years older with her long hair
Shorn by Russian barberesses & skinny male apprentice.
Laura watches skeptically, then
Wants short hair too.
Two babushkas, says a barberess, blushing.
We say thanks, *spasiba*. We pay in roubles, smile,
And walk the decks. At a kiosk: safety pins
And toothpaste. At a coffee lounge: espresso, strong.
Smooth sea, clear sky: you can see for miles.
I think to myself: I am happy.
It is not our lot to be happy. I say to
My wife: though you know that I know it is not our lot
To be happy, today, I say, I am happy.
Today, she says, you are foolish.
Propaganda shorts, punctuated by cartoons,
Begin in the Rainbow Cinema at ten.
Their approach is not unlike my own: This is
The city of Moscow. See the happy people. See them
Work and play. Though we know you know
We know it is not their lot to be happy, today, we say,
They are happy. Today I can almost believe it.
Olga says: Some of you on board
Do evidently take my elementary Russian classes
Lightly. Therefore there will be, she adds,
Examinations. Rossiya, we learn today,
Is from Slavonic
Rus or Ros
Which is from Rutosi which is Finnish
Meaning Swedes
A corruption for the Swedish Rothsmenn
Meaning seamen meaning rowers
Meaning rowers rowing
Seamen

Back to Rothsmenn
To Rutosi Russ or Ross
Slavonic Rossiya. We continue. We row on.
Though we're not permitted visits to the engine room
We are very welcome, thank you, in the galley.
Why, I wonder, as we gaze upon
The shining copper bottoms of the many pots and pans.
Our master cook is called Natasha. First assistant: Fred.
Says Natasha brightly: *SUP n'i-da-SO-l'in*:
There is too little salt in the soup.
Gangs of rival youths, the spoiled sons
Of diplomatic families, East & West, cavort in narrow
Hallways, make a passage dangerous.
We disapprove of gangs of rival youths. We approve
Of peaceful placid crossings always in all seasons yes indeed
And fully air conditioned, stabilized.
We disapprove: of television, of atomic power,
Of planes. We approve: of solar energy, of poetry,
Of ships. Beep beeps of daily news
Are amplified through all the hidden speakers in the walls.
There's no escaping it, nor the *Aurora*, tabloid version
Of the same. Reagan shouts: Remember the Main.
(Does he know about the Storozhevoy?)
In the Commons, fisticuffs; the Pound is down
To one point six. Carter's got his democratic delegates:
He'll win the nomination. Ford will have to fight.
We disapprove: of Carter, Ford, and Reagan. We approve:
Of George the Third and Pitt.
Up on deck again. Sea gulls off the stern:
There must be islands near. At our feet, heavy ropes
And chains for tying up in ports.
Cynouai sights serpent which she likens unto lobster.
Balistae, she has read, threw Regulus his army
At such an awesome shape as this.
She quotes us Olaus Magnus: ". . . . rising like a mast
And eating sheep and swine disturbing ships
And snapping angry men from slippery decks . . ."
Cynouai's developed in the last two years

Some devastating Indiana playground jive – charms
And spells & incantations – which, lamentably,
She teaches gentle Laura. Their poetry
Is ancient and confounding: it ruins equally the
Innocent and guilty, wrecking the unwary.
They smile sweetly at the little boy at lunch
Who has expressed enthusiasm for his broccoli.
"So, so, suck your toe!/All the way to Mexico!"
He pales and expires in his parents' arms.
We vainly offer consolation.
Who among the passengers, we wonder,
Represents the K.G.B.?
Shall we forgive the K.G.B. its agent
On our ship? That wizard in the game room
Taking on all comers at the chess board,
That's the one. Or the strange aristocratic
Lady we discovered after midnight
On the upper deck where animals are kept in kennels
Who was feeding her pet bat.
I notice on a printout that the management
Declines to be responsible
For Acts of God or Piracy (that's fair);
Or for quarantines and seizures, strikes
And "latent vice." They reserve the right
To "land" us if the Captain thinks we are obnoxious
Or unfit. So says clause fourteen;
And I wonder how obnoxious we can get before
We're landed, how they make that nice
Distinction about latent vice.
After lunch, the girls swim.
I talk a while to Brad, a Unitarian from Cleveland,
About sin. I complete some customs forms
And see the big-armed baggage boss. I think of
Olga Korbut, do some exercises in the gym.
Deckspiele, Bridgespiele, if we want to play,
Can bring us prizes: Russian furs
And Balalaikas for the winners. Tea is in
The Vostok Lounge today. Dancing lessons are at four.

The little tailor promises to press
Diana's wrinkled evening dress.
Our Master, Aram M. Oganov, cordially invites us
To attend a formal cocktail party
In the Large Saloon where he will introduce
His senior colleagues late this afternoon. The orchestra
Will play, and Leonid Bozokovich will sing.
Mihail Lermontov, will they recite your poems?
I doubt it, friend. The Baltic Shipping Company and crew
Don't know your stuff, I fear, though
Curiously enough they still have uses for a poet's
Name and legend in the end.
The legend is extreme.
When you died, the locals exorcized your house.
The incense suffocated every flea & louse.
Terrified,
They thought you were demonic.
But you were only just
                    a little bit
                          Byronic.

Seven

My sympathy extends to Lord George-Brown whose photograph is printed in *Aurora* having toppled over in the street outside the B.B.C. in London where he had appeared, more than just a little drunk, to be interviewed and to destroy, before the grinding cameras, his Labour Party card. He was very moved, he said, to do this thing. Then he slipped and fell.

Once I met George Brown, when he was Foreign Secretary, at a party given by my future in-laws shortly after I'd been smitten by the beauty, brains, and grace of a certain elegant Miss Adams. In heady company, in the middle of the mythic Sixties, a decade when intensities were commonplace and inspiration was the rule, my head made light, my tongue made loose by many minty gins, I asked Miss A. to marry me. That I had a wife at home already didn't, at the time, seem to be a complication. I was moved, I said, like Lord George-Brown, to do this thing. Then I slipped and fell.

A few months earlier, Diana blew her interview with M.I.5. What can you do, after all, with a degree in Russian from an English Tech if you're fastidious and will not spy? Her regular attendance at the London branch of the Russian Orthodox Church, as girl chorister, alarmed them as they positively vetted her. She sang, angelic, with a group of ancient (indeed Tzarist) emigrés she'd met at Holborn College. But, ah! who else, wondered M.I.5, might one meet at such a place of dubious repute and mysteries? Their suspicions ended abruptly what might have proved to be a distinguished career. Diana was a pious sort for a while, and took me off to what we later started calling "smells and bells." Once in an endless Sunday mass I scribbled in frustration on an envelope: "O Flaming Slavic God, I pray / Cooperate with me today / Undo this chastity, I say!" It was January, then, of 1967. It took Him roughly until May. . . .

Eight

Hydrodynamics, brother:
waves, and what? makes? waves?
Who or how, then, poets,
oh! the ships. Of similitude
and crest lines, cusps:
We sing it, Mihail Yurievich,
together, no?
For English *scip*, sir,
German *schiff*: all root-like *skap*
I deal I dig out *scoop*:
Scop, we say it, lad, and
ship-shape: poet!
who hath scope enough?
by means of which (of whom) doth
man contrive, convey himself & goods upon
the waves, who waves at
signals lovingly what wives
await returning man he
shanty sings of sea-born signs
Armada Ajax Agamemnon
lo! Renoun or Devastation, *ho* –
Potemkin Homer Mayakovsky
Virgil quote: "Then
first the rivers hollowed alders felt!"

But what? makes waves? components
of Resistance: poets
must, as ships do, dear, encounter
counter, count on it:
so resonant these waves
this hull our hallmark, helmsman –
Red or restive
forces vary as their masses
Newton said of similitude a principle
vouchsafe it I to
poets ships of state or captains

legislators unacknowledged
wonder (I do) *could* you, Lermontov,
have suffered out an exile
in "The West?"
In my America, "America"
in circumstances
we could hypothetically
imagine for you
tired and poor
and brave
and staring down some shitfaced
bureaucrat who couldn't
spell your name
on Ellis Island though it
wouldn't have been
Ellis Island then, not yet?
Instead of death at 26
an immigration
maybe
to ByGod ByGum
your ship against
our waves
your waves against
our shores
resistance or combustion and collapse?

Napoleon abdicates
and Washington burns down.
Clay, Calhoun
and Crawford clamour.
Madison makes war.
Who'd mediate with Castlereagh?
Who'd cluck: "The Tzar?"
Commission oh commissioner it's
Adams fast and far.
Francis Key goes spangley in a decent dawn.
Thornton saves the patents.
You blink

at Moscow midwives
and you learn to say: Tarhani.
Your generation's made superfluous
in Russia by
the poet-peacock's frenzy
of December '25: the profiles
of the hanged
bleed into the margins of *Onegin*.
As the dandy and the duelist
replace the likes of
Kuchelbecker and Kondraty Ryleev,
the Masons go all misty
and Mickiewicz cries: despair.

Do I see you as a Locofoco candidate?
An alien-seditious Natty Bumppo
tough enough to topple even Tammany?
Or Bard of Biddle's Bank?
Cousin, your ambivalence about all things
matches even mine: –
You take, I think,
no Hannibalic oath with Herzen.

On the Wabash, maybe,
some reformer leads you
as a pre-pubescent
to anticipate Pechorin's adolescence
with the Shaker image
of a rehabilitated bum
coined in Owen's dialogues
with Adams & Monroe:
A Hero Of Our Time in Indiana,
positive & realist,
wrought to win in 1841
the Brook Farm Fourier award,
wrought to win
the distant praises of Zhadanov.

"Oh the plundered plowman
and the beggared
yeomanry," quoth Jefferson
who never really cared about
the buggered beggers –
And old John Randolph said: "it's
a stinking coalition now
of Blifil and Black George!"
Bargain and intrigue, he meant,
between the Nullifiers
and the Feds.
Though you were only twelve,
who hath scope enough?
In time, perhaps,
you'd be a good Jacksonian:
A kitchen-cabinet member
cribbing notes from Crockett
pilfering from Poe
dreaming of Tecumseh's ghost
and Lake Ontario
as you give your arm, chivalrous,
to the blemished Peg O'Neale,
write your epic *Alamo*
and draft at last a swan song
in your famous
ode: "Hypothicated Bonds."

In 1837, with the Panic,
you take off:
The West! You write to Mme. Arsenieva
née Stolypin: "The Rockies
are my Caucasus in exile:
who hath scope enough?" And of
the river boats: "*The means!* by which
a man contrives –
conveys himself and goods
upon the waves . . ."
All the rest is lost in mountain mists

and in
the numberless lacunae
which I find
in Olga's reading lists.

Oh, you were born beneath a curious star.
Who'd mediate with Castlereagh
would cluck: "The Tzar."
I whisper in your dreamy ear
babushka
in your favorite hatch.

We heave most handily past headlands toward the Thames.

**Nine: A Conclusion of The Mihail Lermontov Poems
beginning with documentation, paraphrase, and quotations
taken down in the Revolutionary Reading Room from a
fine old tome on the Thames by Allen Wykes and ending by
way of a change, once again, of my name . . .**

At the other end of the river, at the other end of time, they offer
sacrifices to the Great God Lud: a bevy of virgins is flushed
down the spring at Lechlade where the River God and his
friends – who much prefer the virgins to the sheep and roosters
which they sometimes get instead, a substitution which, as we
can easily imagine, often leads to wicked floods in the Spring –
run (says my authority) *a pumping station belching out the daily fifteen
hundred million gallons of water* pouring toward us even now over
the weir at Teddington as we flow west with the tide toward
Tilbury. *Hic tuus O Tamisine Pater septemgeminus fons*: "Here, O
Father Thames, is your sevenfold fount." Among the
potamologists, in fact, there is no agreement as to exactly where
it is. But Leche will do for us as it did for Drayton in his
Polyolbion, as it did for his friend Shipton when he found in
Trewsbury Mede that "no water floweth hereabouts til Leche,
the onlie true begetter."

If to my starboard red appear
    It is my duty to keep clear;
Act as judgement says is proper
    Port or starboard –
Back or stop her . . .

None of your *Wallala-leialalas* for us; that's a boatman's song
with a social function to perform. Not so long ago the captains
of ships mismanaged by members of the lively fraternity
operating out of Gravesend under the Ruler of Pilots were
encouraged to dispatch on the spot any incompetent or unlucky
helmsman with appropriate ceremonials or without. We've
flown our yellow Q and blue and orange stripes; we've blown an
angry short and two long blasts on our horn and taken on our
pilot from the pilot cutter. He sings his lonely song: *But when*

upon my port is seen/a steamer's starboard light of green,/For me there's nought to do or see/that green to port keeps clear of me. So we are now in the hands of a specialist in rivers and can hope, muttering whatever spells or mnemonics we like, to reach our proper berth with no encounters along the way with any supertankers, QE 2s, ghostly Kelmscott oarsmen, estuary chains, Gordon fortifications, sunken Armadas, lightships, sands, sheers, nesses, muds, or stone outcroppings along the Hundred of Hoo. The statue of Pocahontas, who never made it home, stares at us through a Dickensian fog.

"His body doth incarnadine," remarked a jailor, "Thamesis to uncommon sanguine beauty." It was a notable execution. If Thames Head is hard to find – whether in the Mede or in the Leche or in the Pool at Seven Springs – the Thames heads are far too numerous to count. I see them vividly before me bobbing in our wake, all those lovely saints and sinners, chatting with each other about noble or ignoble deeds, drifting toward Westminster with the tide. That it should have been the *head* that always so offended! Why not, like Montezuma, pluck out hearts? No, the English god did not want hearts; you lose your head or mind in this cold country, or you hang. Your heart is yours for hoarding. Said the Virgin Queen, keeping hers to herself, red of wig and black of tooth, Tilbury protectress – "I have the heart and stomach of a king!" The pirate Drake prepared once more to burn the Spanish beard: – *with*
further protestatione that if wants
of victualles and munitione were suppliede we wold
pursue them to the furthese
that they durste
have gone . . .
A less official pirate, late of Scotland, said most memorably upon espying, there on execution dock, a friend: "I've lain the bitch three times and now she comes to see me hanged!" Three tides washed the bones; then he waved for days from Bugsby's Reach. . . . Tippling pints in Whitby's Prospect or in Ramsgate's Town we think we'd like it better in the past. When they flushed the virgins down the drain at Leche, floated heads

in rivers or impaled them ornamentally on pikes – when oh they
hung the pirates low beneath the tide. We'd drink we would
we'd
go pursue them durste
supply the victualles and munitione
write immortal doggerel we'd fight for Gloriana
Boudicca Victoria Regina choose your time
by Kitchener do your bit
for Winston spot the doodlebugs and buzzbombs
pluck out mines off Cliffe
outfox De Ruyter beat that prick Napoleon
prop on some dark night
a poor unlucky scapegoat in the new foundations my fair lady
of the bridge
and bind him there
we'd set a man to watch all night we'd do the job ourselves.
But you do not choose your time.

Lucky, guilty –
exiled or pursued,
some can choose at least a place.
As the times impinged
obscurely, George Learmont abandoned Thomas Rhymer's
tower and – as mercenary, pirate – left his home and went to
organize the cavalry in Poland for a minor Tzar. His business
there was doubtless foul. Later, Mihail Yurievich would dream
of heather, kilts, and thistles, dream of George Learmont,
dream of ancestors and Malcolm and MacBeth as time – his
times – impinged on him obscurely, making him superfluous,
sending him to the Dragoons and to the mountains where he
prophesied his end, with great precision, twice. He "eloquently
yearned," a learned scholar writes, quoting his worst stuff,
"to fly to high and misty crags and wake the wild harp of
Scotland once again." But the Russian god, unlike the English,
wanted hearts, great hearts – Lermontov's and Pushkin's – a
nasty bullet through each one. The Russian god would make of
both a statue and a ship – machinery converting poetry to prose,
roubles into dollars, treaties into grain, and revolution into

resolutions and détente. Because of which we may avoid a
holocaust and bore each other to our graves.

For my time, too, impinges oddly,
painlessly, obscurely – this kind of inbetween –
impinges surely
this time of jokes & parodies, pastiches.
An inbetween
when I don't know precisely what I want to do in time
but only where I want to go
again –
And so we're here and waiting
for a berth
to park a ship in –
waiting in a time of waiting

A time of wating for –
For semi-retired former semi-active veteran-volunteers
of oh our still belovèd
dear and hopeful
sixties
to arise again arise
again arise
For some kind fool to build the equestrian statues
and compose the elegiac songs.

Riding high and mightily on weary white lame mare
whose forelegs beat the air
and haunches heave
his head at a tilt, his purple plumèd hat all brandishèd
on high on high
on point of keen upraisèd terrible swift sword
Squadron Leader Jack Arzeno-Kirkpatrick
sings his able arias
in honour of Air Vice-Marshal Matthias –
who has children
and a wife
who is middle class for life.

Said Marx (correctly):
men will make their history, all right,
but not exactly
as they think or choose.
(Even he had everything to lose
with that excuse.)

The signal flags unfurl and fly;
the lights flash on.
Down come blue and orange stripes,
the yellow Q:
Up go W and L, and
up goes V:
Have you got dead rats on board?
Answers ATI: *There is no cause for alarm.*
BCV replies: *Approved.*
Down come quickly *rats, no cause, approved* –
Up goes HKB:
*Hello, Komsomolka: I want
to ask you a question. Is gallantry obsolete?*
Flaps the dreaded Drake: *Think, by god,
of the Queen.* Down with HKB
and Drake, up with
M. Maksimich: *Was it the French who invented
the fashion of being bored?*
We fly the blue Pechorin: *No, it was the English.*
Taking our various oaths, we resolve
to be gallant again, and brave –
yes, Komsomolskaya –
and away with Boredom, England!
We fly *The Plundered Plowman.*
We will not plunder –
we'll plow.
We fly *The Beggared Yeoman.*
We will not beggar
we'll yodel.
*And there's a kind of waterish Tree at Wapping
whereas sea-thieves
or pirates are catched napping.*

Oh, our resolutions are serious enough
in spite of the jokes
and in spite of our preoccupations
– the baggage, the passports –
and we really do propose to lead a better life this year
than last
though we do not tell ourselves exactly how.

Standing on the promenade
in attitudes
of suspicion, attention, or anticipation
hoping for some fine
benign surprise
each of us looks at the land
thinking still of the sea.
Each contrives
to be abstracted one last time in sea-thoughts
or in dreams
before the symbolical stranger
posing as a customs agent
or a clerk or porter in a small hotel or pension
asks the question symbolical strangers ask
which only actions answer

and each, I think, hums a variation
on the final chorus
of the tune
– changing names and faces,
touching all the graces –
that he's whistled up and down the decks
through afternoon & afternoon.

– O wild Italian-Irish Lass & Muse
protect with sprezzatura
and some Gaelic gall this voyager
his life
his children and his wife.
O help me take off my disguise.

Help to make me good
and wise.
I've been to God and man
Jack Arzeno-Kirkpatrick
for an odd span
of days
of days and nights.

Bibliographical Note

I am indebted, as in *Turns* and *Bucyrus*, to an odd assortment of books and authors for facts, fancies, passages of verse or of prose, translations, information, scholarship and scandal which I have had occasion in these poems to quote, plagiarize, willfully ignore, tactfully modify, stupidly misconstrue, or intentionally travesty. The debts are as follows: (1) In *The Stefan Batory Poems*: Adam Mickiewicz, *Pan Tadeusz* (in the G. R. Noyes translation); *Adam Mickiewicz* (Unesco Books: essays by several hands); V. L. Benes and N. J. G. Pounds, *Poland*; Tadeusz Ocioszynski, *Poland on the Baltic*; Jerzy Jan Lerski, *A Polish Chapter in Jacksonian America*; Henry Beston, *The St. Lawrence*; Guilbert Parker and Claude G. Bryan, *Old Quebec*; Eric Zagrans, two rejected lines from an early draft of his translation into Yiddish of "The Love Song of J. Alfred Prufrock." (2) In *The Mihail Lermontov Poems: The Poetry of Lermontov* (edited and translated by C. E. l'Ami); *A Lermontov Reader* (edited and translated by Guy Daniels); Mihail Lermontov, *A Hero of our Time* (in the Nabokov translation); Janko Lavrin, *Lermontov*; Serge Sovietov, *Mickiewicz in Russia*; Edward J. Brown, *Russian Literature Since the Revolution*; Yon Barna, *Eisenstein*; Colette Shulman, ed., *We the Russians*; James H. Billington, *The Icon and the Axe*; Robert Payne, *The Fortress*; Charles M. Wiltse, *The New Nation*; R. C. McGrane, *The Panic of 1837*; N. K. Risjord, *The Old Republicans*; Sir Edward Creasy, *15 Decisive Battles*; Alan Wykes, *An Eye on the Thames*; Basil E. Cracknell, *Portrait of London River*; Philip Howard, *London's River*; A. P. Herbert, *The Thames*. (3) In the short poems of sections I and II: Johan Huizinga, *Homo Ludens*; *The Manual of Horsemanship of the British Horse Society and Pony Club*; Lars Noren, "Autumn"; tags from Robert Lowell, John Berryman, W. B. Yeats, Woody Allen, Robert Hass, Wordsworth, *King Lear*, Mark Twain, Paul Verlaine, Rudyard Kipling, Edmund Burke; Bryan Houghton, *Saint Edmund, King and Martyr; Proceedings of the Suffolk Institute of Archaeology for 1969*; Enid Porter, *The Folklore of East Anglia*; C. J. Stranks, *St. Etheldreda: Queen and Abbess*; *The Book of Margery Kempe* (translated by W. Butler-Bowdon with an introduction by R. W. Chambers); Justin Kaplan, *Mr. Clemens and Mark Twain*; Mark Twain, "The Celebrated Jumping Frog of Calavaras County"; Joanna Richardson, *Verlaine*; Paul Verlaine, *Sagesse*; Joan Poulson, *Old Anglian Recipes*; Richard Cobbold, *The History of Margaret Catchpole*; W. G. Arnott, *Orwell Estuary*; Julian Tennyson, *Suffolk Scene*; George Ewart Evans, *Ask the Fellows Who Cut the Hay*; Julian of

Norwich, *Revelations of Divine Love* (in the Clifton Wolters translation);
P. Franklin Chambers, *Juliana of Norwich: an Introductory Appreciation
and an Interpretive Anthology*; R. A. Edwards, *The Fighting Bishop*; R. B.
Dobson, ed., *The Peasants' Revolt of 1381*; Rodney Hilton, *Bond Men
Made Free;* Norman Cohn, *The Pursuit of the Millennium.*

Much of the material I have made use of, especially in the two longish
comic sequences, is merely a matter of schoolboy history. However,
the mid-Atlantic nature of these poems makes for a problem: it all
depends on where you went to school. American readers may not
recognize one set of references, English readers may not recognize
another. Of course neither British nor American readers will
necessarily recognize the Polish and Russian references. My editor, after
some perplexity among reviewers of my last book *Turns*, suggested
more extensive notes for *Crossing*. Though I have decided to restrict
them, as before, to a bibliography, I will add here what might be an
example of a "more extensive note" to one of the shorter poems in
order to suggest, if nothing else, what questions of length, expense,
and ugliness are involved. Only David Jones has really mastered the art
of opening up "unshared backgrounds" – or even, as one must now
say, "unshared foregrounds" – in notes. The following was put
together for a BBC broadcast of "26 June 1381/1977." "Henry
Despenser (or le Despenser, or Lespenser – the name is given a French
pronunciation in the seventeenth line) was Bishop of Norwich during
the period of the Peasants' Revolt and put down an East Anglian
version of that insurrection in the fields of North Walsham on 26 June
1381. The leader of the Norfolk revolt, Geoffrey Lidster (or Litster, or
Litester), a dyer by trade, was defeated, tried, and confessed by
Despenser, who then followed him as he was dragged behind a wagon
to the place of execution, trying to keep the condemned man's head
from bouncing on the road. For putting down the revolt the Norfolk
nobles gave Despenser the famous painted retable, or reredos, now in
Norwich Cathedral, which was restored by Pauline Plummer in 1958.
The poem has to do with the revolt, the execution of Lidster, the
painting of the reredos, the restoration of the reredos, and with
various reactions to these events. A fragment from one of the
allegorical letters of protest which circulated during the Peasants'
Revolt is quoted in the poem, as is the well-known rhyme of the period
about Adam and Eve. Though in point of historical fact Despenser's
brass has disappeared, we know that the epitaph included the words

miles amatus and *boni pastoris mens* – "beloved soldier" and "the soul of this good shepherd." I should perhaps add, by way of introduction, that malachite and azurite were used in the restoration of the anonymous Norwich master's painting of the last events in the life of Christ, and that the restorer had to replace entirely the head and arms of Christ on the cross in the wooden center panel."

Acknowledgements

Many of these poems have been published previously. Grateful acknowledgement is made to *The Times Literary Supplement* for "Friendship"; to *Encounter* for "In Memory of the American Fifties"; to *Encounter* and *A Tumult for John Berryman* for "A Reply"; to *Bennington Review* for "Brandon, Breckland: The Flint Knappers"; to *Bennington Review* and *PN Review* for "From A Visit to Dalmatia"; to *PN Review* for "Poem for Cynouai", "Dunwich: Winter Visit Alone", "Two Ladies", "Verrucas" (which appeared, together with "Two Ladies", as "Three Ladies"), "59 Lines Assembled Quickly Sitting on a Wall Near the Reconstruction of the Lady Juliana's Cell", and "26 June 1381/1977"; to *PN Review* and *The New Review* for section Six of "The Stefan Batory Poems" (which appeared as "Mid-Atlantic: Night"); to *PN Review*, *Perfect Bound* and the Sceptre Press pamphlet series for "After the Death of Chekhov"; to the Sceptre Press pamphlet series for "You Measure John"; to *Poetry Wales* for "On Lake Michigan – I"; to *Poetry Wales* and *Heartland II* for "On Lake Michigan – II"; to *Poetry Wales* and *Salmagundi* for "In Columbus, Ohio"; to *Salmagundi* for "U.S.I.S. Lecturer"; to *Salmagundi* and the B.B.C. (*Poetry Now*) for "On the Death of Benjamin Britten"; to *TriQuarterly* for sections One through Ten of "The Stefan Batory Poems"; to *The New Review* for sections One and Three of "The Mihail Lermontov Poems"; to *The Greenfield Review* for "The Fen Birds' Cry" and "Evening Song".